Butterfly Kisses & Bittersweet Tears

◇ ◇ ◇ ◇ ◇ ◇ ◇ ◇ ◇ ◇

Stories of
Fathers & Daughters
Told to and by
BOB CARLISLE

WORD PUBLISHING
Nashville·London·Vancouver·Melbourne

BOB CARLISLE
BUTTERFLY KISSES

Published by Word Publishing,
a division of Thomas Nelson, Inc., Nashville, TN 37214

Library of Congress Cataloging-in-Publication Data
Carlisle, Bob, 1956–
A collection of butterfly kisses : stories of fathers and
daughters told to and by Bob Carlisle / Bob Carlisle.
p.   cm.
ISBN 0-8499-1339-X
1. Fathers and daughters—Fiction. I. Title.
PS3553.A7176C6   1998
813'.54—dc21
97-46460
CIP

Printed in the United States of America
8 9 0 1 2 3 4 5 6 BVG 9 8 7 6 5 4 3 2 1

There's two things I know for sure:
She was sent here from heaven,
and she's Daddy's little girl.
As I drop to my knees by her bed at night,
she talks to Jesus, and I close my eyes.
And I thank God for all the joy in my life,
but most of all for . . .

Butterfly Kisses after bedtime prayer.
Stickin' little white flowers all up in her hair.
"Walk beside the pony, Daddy; it's my first ride."
"I know the cake looks funny, Daddy,
but I sure tried."
Oh, with all that I've done wrong,
I must have done something right
to deserve a hug every morning
and Butterfly Kisses at night.

Sweet sixteen today,
she's looking like her momma
a little more every day.
One part woman, the other part girl.
To perfume and makeup,
from ribbons and curls.
Trying her wings out in a great big world.
But I remember . . .

Butterfly Kisses after bedtime prayer.
Stickin' little white flowers all up in her hair.
"You know how much I love you, Daddy,
but if you don't mind, I'm only going
to kiss you on the cheek this time."
With all that I've done wrong,

I must have done something right
to deserve her love every morning,
and Butterfly Kisses at night.
All the precious time
like the wind, the years go by.
Preciously butterfly
spread your wings and fly.

She'll change her name today.
She'll make a promise, and I'll give her away.
Standing in the bride room just staring at her,
she asked me what I'm thinking
and I said, "I'm not sure.
I just feel like I'm losing my baby girl."
Then she leaned over and gave me . . .

Butterfly Kisses, with her momma there.
Stickin' little white flowers all up in her hair.
"Walk me down the aisle, Daddy,
it's just about time."
"Does my wedding gown look pretty, Daddy?
"Daddy don't cry."
With all that I've done wrong,
I must have done something right
to deserve her love every morning,
and Butterfly Kisses . . .

I couldn't ask God for more,
man, this is what love is.
I know I've gotta let her go,

but I'll always remember . . .
Every hug in the morning
and Butterfly Kisses . . .

Dear Reader,

Since the song "Butterfly Kisses" was first introduced, I've been overwhelmed with responses from dads, daughters, moms, best friends, boyfriends, grandparents, and countless other listeners who have been deeply touched by the song's lyrics. As letters poured in to us from all around the world, we began to envision a way of making the stories they tell available to everyone.

Our first step was to set up our Internet website, www.bobcarlisle.com, so the messages could be read and responded to. But everybody isn't online, and people continue to write to our office, send notes to us at concerts, and communicate with our publishers. And the more we heard, the more we realized that these letters, both online and through the mail, contained a wealth of wisdom, invaluable life-lessons, and priceless memories.

Some of these letters were roughly crafted in the handwriting of men and women who are unpolished in their writing skills. Some were hurriedly typed on a computer keyboard. Some came from highly educated correspondents and were meticulously worded. Some were heartlifting, and others were heartbreaking. Many of the writers were uncomfortable providing us with their identities or locations. In fact, there were those who didn't even sign their names.

In order to create this book, we have selected sixty-two of the most compelling stories we've received. We've rewritten them, and at times we've combined them. All of the stories you'll read are true, but we've chosen to fictionalize certain aspects and details of them in order to protect the people who shared them.

Our hope is that you will be as touched as we've been by the fathers and daughters you'll meet on the pages that follow. They are from very different back-grounds and experiences, yet they mirror aspects of all of our lives. The love they describe is a universal and God-given love, shared by fathers and their daughters everywhere. I'm convinced that there's no love quite like it in the entire world.

Bob Carlisle

Part 1

There's two things I know for sure:
She was sent here from heaven, and she's Daddy's
little girl.

⌒

Our daughters are very precious gifts from above. We'd have to be blind not to see the master hand at work in their conception, their birth, and their growing up.

Some of the *Butterfly Kisses* stories we've received are from fathers who have been spiritually touched and blessed by their daughters' lives. Other stories are from daughters who have seen, directly or indirectly, something of their Heavenly Father's love in the lives of their dads.

Sometimes the stories are happy ones, where grace is evident and prayers are miraculously answered. And sometimes the stories are painful, and we struggle to make sense of the pain. In any case, one thing is clear: daughters really are sent from heaven. Dads and daughters are brought closer to each other and closer to heaven by the unfolding events of their lives and by the love they share for each other.

*M*y father looks a little different from other men. That's because his face is scarred. He was burned badly in a fire when he was a little boy, and his face was affected more than any other part of his body. At the time, doctors took skin from his stomach and grafted it on his face in order to cover the terrible burns. Eventually he healed, but not without a lot of pain, and a lifetime of disfigurement.

Because of his own suffering, Dad could never tolerate hearing us kids make fun of other people. He would send us to our rooms with no dinner if he heard us laughing at other children for being "different." When I was really little, I never understood his sensitivity, because I was used to the way he looked, and it never occurred to me that he had faced terrible mocking and meanness as he grew up.

But when I was in high school, my face broke out with acne. I was so depressed that I didn't want to go to school in the mornings, and sometimes when I got home in the afternoon I just wanted to close myself in my room and cry. One day Dad sat down next to me on the couch, looked at my face, and gently ran his rough fingers across my broken out skin.

"Why does it have to be like this?" I burst out.

He shook his head sadly. "I don't know," he said again and again, so softly I could hardly hear him. He put his strong arms around me and held me while I wept, and he prayed that God would help me get better and be strong. When I finally stopped crying, I looked up at him. His scarred face was wet. He'd been crying, too.

M. R.,
Hutchinson, KS

$\mathcal{T}$he first time we saw my daughter, she was sitting alone in an orphanage crib. We were touring an Eastern European country where thousands of parentless children were institutionalized, and parents sometimes even abandoned their children in shabby state-run facilities. This child was silent and still, and her eyes were huge and empty. She wasn't quite two years old and, for some reason, she looked like she belonged in our family.

My wife and I had three children of our own—all boys—and we had always wanted a daughter. The moment we caught sight of this sick and lonely child, we just looked at each other. We both knew immediately what we wanted to do. We wrote down her name, all the essential information, and before we left, I asked if we could hold her. As I picked her up, I was shocked by her feathery lightness. She was pathetically thin, and her body felt as if it had no substance. She was completely passive. She allowed us to hold her and didn't pull away, but she seemed completely unable to respond to our love.

Before the day was over, we began to inquire about the necessary paper work for adoption. While we went through the motions, we spent most of our energy talking and trying to be sure we were doing the right thing. Our boys were at home with their grandparents—they were six, eight, and eleven years old. For a year, they'd been asking us for a sister. We phoned home and told them about the little girl. "I've been praying for a sister," my youngest told me. "Maybe this is the answer."

Naturally, we wanted to take her home with us, but the red tape was frustratingly long, complicated, and expensive. By the time we left the country, discouragement was beginning to creep into our hearts. Maybe it was just a crazy idea. We got home, and life went on as if nothing had happened. We called our contacts there each week, but there was no news. We resigned ourselves to disappointment, and tried to figure out how to get the boys to stop praying.

Then, after three full months had passed with no change in the circumstances, a call came to us from a church near the orphanage where we'd left the case in the hands of a local attorney. "Come and get her," the woman told us. "Everything has been approved."

We booked our flight with both joy and apprehension. Questions began to torment our minds. How serious were her health problems? How emotionally damaged was she? What if the boys didn't accept her wholeheartedly? A thousand questions, and no answers except one came to us: "This is the daughter you asked for."

Once she was in our home, our newly adopted child started to change almost immediately. With good nutrition and proper medical care, she began to eat, and little by little she grew bigger and stronger. As days and weeks passed, she learned how to hug us when we held her. Eventually, she reached out her arms to us, and we noticed that her eyes had begun to sparkle. One day, about a month after her arrival, she smiled. And to my great delight, she smiled at me—her adopted Daddy. I started to cry, and so did my wife.

It's hard to describe how much I love my boys. They are part of my wife and me, physically, emotion-ally, and spiritually. But this little girl—she's now six years old, the best reader in her class, and a dynamite soccer player—holds a part of my heart that no one else can touch. She is courageous, she is strong, and she is beautiful. Her three big brothers treat her like gold. Her mother says she's her "pride and joy." But to me, most of all, she is a miracle. Our daughter is a living testimony to the power of love, and how it can bring health and hope and happiness to the most hopeless little child.

S. H.,
Akron, OH

*J*t's funny—with my dad it seems like it's the smallest things I remember best. When I was growing up, my dad wasn't one to give a lot of sympathy for all the little scrapes and hurts and bruises, so I always went to my mom for that kind of thing. She was really tenderhearted and I knew if I got hurt, she'd not only bandage me, but she'd give me a hug and a little extra dessert after dinner.

In the same situation, Dad would have shrugged, told me to put a Band-Aid on it, and sent me back outside to play.

My mother's tenderheartedness extended to her parents, and when my grandmother became chronically ill, Mom was there to care for her whenever it was possible. Unfortunately, on the same day I had to have my wisdom teeth pulled, Grandma fell and hurt herself pretty badly. I wasn't too happy to hear that my Dad would be taking care of me after the oral surgery!

I got in the car with him, my face stuffed with gauze, tears streaming from my eyes. I was really hurting. I headed for my room once we got home and was amazed to find Dad walking right there beside me, holding my arm in case I was lightheaded from the anesthesia. He sat me down on my bed and helped me change into my nightgown. He propped me up in bed, turned on the TV, handed me the channel changer, and told me he'd be right back. Miserable as I felt, I could hardly believe this was my Dad, actually babying me. And he wasn't finished.

After he left me in my room, I heard a lot of noise and racket in the kitchen, and then he reappeared with a milkshake he'd made for me. An hour later he was back with my pain medication. He checked on me all afternoon and evening, and he was there when I woke up the next morning, making sure I had slept alright.

He made me scrambled eggs and brought them to me with apple sauce, so I wouldn't have to chew anything.

This went on for two days—literally the whole weekend. By the time Mom got home, I was one hundred percent better. When I tried to thank Dad and to explain how nice I thought he'd been, he said, "What did you expect?"

I didn't dare tell him, because I realized that I'd just gotten to know him in a whole new way. I decided that he's kind of like God—he's there when you really need him.

W. E.,
Rock Hill, SC

*M*y firstborn son died of cancer when he was six years old, after a long and painful ordeal. Afterward, my wife and I did our best to get on with our lives. First of all, our son had a little sister who needed us. And besides, we were both working toward Ph.D. degrees. We tried to lose ourselves in our daughter, our studies, and ourselves. We soon had two more children, and we made every effort to love them wholeheartedly and to leave our little lost boy in God's hands.

My response to the tragedy was to return to my Christian faith. My wife chose other alternatives—she committed herself to sociology and feminism, and ultimately turned her back on her faith altogether. Over the years, the spiritual gulf between us became immense, and my wife finally decided to turn her back on us, too. She left the children with me and went out on her own.

The rejection the children experienced was indescribable. And my own sense of loss and depression was overwhelming. How could I possibly care for my children with the kind of love and devotion they needed? They were so fragile, so precious, and so young. How could they ever understand? For that matter, how could I?

One day my youngest daughter brought me a verse from Sunday school. "Daddy, I think you'll like this one," she said and smiled, looking as if she knew something I didn't.

As I read the words, I felt as if they had been written especially for me. The passage was like a love letter from God Himself. It not only told me how to continue to care for my children, but it gave me a perspective about my life that I'd never had before: "Trust in the LORD with all your heart, And lean not on your own understanding; In all your ways

acknowledge Him, And He shall direct your paths"
(Proverbs 3:5–6).

Up until that day, I had always relied on my
personal intelligence and wisdom to see me through.
Now, for the first time, I knew that I wasn't on my
own, trying to care for my children by my wits. A
wiser mind than mine, and a far more loving heart
than mine had taken charge of our family. Now, at
last, I could let go.

V. H.,
Pendleton, OR

*O*ne of the most important days of my life is about to happen—I'm going to meet my father for the first time. I'm in my thirties, and I've always wondered about him. But a few weeks ago I got a phone call. He had finally tracked me down after years and years of trying. And he's flying to see me. He lives in New England, and I live in Miami. He'll be here this time next week.

There are so many questions in my mind. I know very little about him. He's a college professor, and he is divorced. He and my mother knew each other only briefly, and she found out she was pregnant after he left for Vietnam. He was injured; she fell in love with someone else. They lost contact.

I wonder if I look like him? He's very intelligent, and I hope I can keep up with his thought and ideas.

During the few conversations we've had, I've been really impressed with the things he says and the words he chooses. I'm proud of his accomplishments and excited to think that I'm part of him.

Of course I'm nervous—my husband says it's sort of like a blind date. There are so many different ways people respond to people. Will he be attracted or annoyed? Will he be happy, or wish he hadn't tried to find me? My thoughts and fears are random, and I'm making myself crazy.

The one thing I can say for sure is that I'm so grateful to God that my father cared enough to track me down. He must be a unique person to make all the effort, to care enough to know me, to spend the time and money to meet me face to face. Considering that, and the way he sounds on the phone, I think I'm going to like him a lot. I just hope and pray he likes me too.

C. G.,

Miami, FL

*M*y parents were divorced when I was just two years old, and at that point my "real" father pretty well disappeared from the face of the earth. Meanwhile, Mom married again. And, believe it or not, her new husband married her without ever meeting my sister or me.

It might have been a disaster with any other man, but my stepfather accepted his ready-made new family without a blink. From the moment he first walked through the door, he began to love us wholeheartedly— no matter what we did. I never doubted his love from that day on.

Without question, our most memorable moment occurred when I was sixteen. One afternoon we drove to the restaurant together where I was to meet my "real" father. I remember the sad look in Daddy's eyes (which he tried to hide, but couldn't) while he sat for two hours in a coffee shop booth alone, waiting for me to try and get to know a complete stranger.

It was then and there that I realized how much I loved my "Daddy." No one could make me feel as safe as he did. He was a gift to me, and no one would ever replace him. The unconditional love he had shown me from the day we met had taken root and grown in my heart, too. I knew then that it would last for a lifetime.

A. S.,
Temple, TX

*W*hen doctors announce the birth of a baby, it's usually a happy moment. And my wife and I were ecstatic that our fifth child was the daughter we'd prayed for. But when the doctor approached me after her birth, I knew immediately that something was wrong. "Her heart isn't working properly," he explained. "I suspect a defect of some sort . . ."

She did have a heart defect, and the next few days were so difficult—she barely hung on between life and death for the first week. Then, once that crisis passed, she required three dangerous heart surgeries. We felt like we were gambling with her life every time she went into the operating room. At the time, we were praying as a family day and night, promising God that if he would take care of our daughter's problems, we

19

would be content with whatever else life might bring our way. My four sons, my wife and I laid everything out before God, and pleaded with Him for help.

It seemed like a miracle when my little girl began to improve and, little by little, gained strength and health. She grew up into a beautiful young woman and eventually fell in love and got married. We had been told, during the early years of her struggle, that she would never be able to have children. God miraculously overruled even that—she gave birth to three healthy sons.

But tragedy later struck in a completely different way. My youngest son was suddenly taken from us. He was killed in a hit-and-run accident, and our family was stunned by the loss. There are many mysteries in life, and we could never understand why such a terrible thing should happen. We grieved his loss and wept many tears. But we knew better than to question God's love. We'd promised Him that we would be content, no matter what happened. So we did our best to accept the loss of our dear son and brother, and to be thankful for all the good things in our lives—especially our daughter's miraculous healing and her healthy children.

I don't have answers for those big life questions. Some of them will just have to remain unanswered in this life. But I can give this one important piece of advice to anyone who will listen: Tell your children every day how much they are loved. Make the most of your time with them today. You never know when you won't get the chance again.

B. F.,
Somerset, KY

*M*y daughter is my inspiration. She was just a newborn baby when I was first locked up in this penitentiary, and I am only able to see her on weekends. When she and her mother leave me on Sunday nights, I sometimes sit and cry, remembering the things I have done wrong. Those wrong things I've done have kept me from being with my daughter. And it is my little girl that makes me want to be a different man when I get out of jail.

I've been going to a prison prayer meeting every week, and I'm learning that God can help me change my way of life. My faith gives me hope that I will be a good father to my little girl. She'll be starting school soon, and when I get out of prison, I want to be the kind of dad she needs. I want to play with her and talk to her and help her grow up to be healthy and happy.

She is the reason I'm trying to change and grow. I love her that much.

J. B.,

Eddyville, KY

*A*s a musician, I've been on tour almost as long as I can remember. When my wife and I got married, we knew it wasn't going to be easy to keep our marriage together, but we were determined to try. It wasn't too difficult for me. I missed my wife when I was on the road, but we had great reunions when we got back together. In a way, I guess we got used to it.

But then everything changed. My wife found out she was pregnant, and before we knew it, we had the most beautiful little girl in the world. I already loved my wife with all my heart. Now I felt like I would burst with all the love inside me.

My daughter grew so fast. Every time I came home she was doing something new, and my heart nearly broke because by the time a tour was over, I'd missed a whole stage of her development. Before her birth, I used to go out with the guys once in a while and sometimes I did things I regretted later. But once she came along, I wasn't interested in drinking and messing around. I wanted to be a good father. I was determined to be respectable, and I wanted her to be proud of me. So, I started to pray for wisdom.

This went on for three years. It got harder and harder for me to be away from home, and easier and easier to say no to old habits. Finally, my wife and I made a decision to move to Nashville, where I could perform and still be at home. Today I have the best of both worlds—I'm home during the day, so my little girl and I have lots of time together. When I go out at night to play, she's in bed and never even knows I'm gone.

I think my daughter changed my life in more ways than even I realize. I've grown up and learned that love is more than an emotion. It's a way of living and a reason to be a responsible person. This week my wife and I found out that we're expecting again. I thank

God that he's changed me and made me the kind of father I should be.

D. W.,
Nashville, TN

*W*orld War II was barely over when I got the telegram. My wife of thirteen years wired me urgently in Guam—she had just learned that she was expecting our first child! We had been told time and again that we could not conceive children, and the news was nothing short of a miracle.

But I was on a tour of duty that wouldn't end before the baby's birth. And if there was any place in the world I wanted to be, it was at the U.S. Navy Hospital in San Diego that coming September. There wasn't much I could say to my commanding officer— there were guys with sick parents, guys with broken hearts, guys with bigger problems than mine who wanted to get home. I had men under my command who were pleading with me for furlough. The one thing I knew I could do was pray. And that's what I did.

One night, aboard ship, the desire to get home to

my wife lay heavy on my heart. I was on night watch, and as the hours ticked by, I paced the deck, talking to God. I was pretty much by myself, and toward the end of the watch I knelt in prayer. As I prayed, the anxiety and discontentment I had felt since my wife's telegram began to fade. Instead, I felt a sense of peace and joy. Though I dearly wanted to be with my wife during this precious time, somehow I felt content and I was sure that my prayers had been heard.

Forty-eight hours later, I heard my name at mail call. I recognized at once that the letter for me was from the Naval base in San Diego. With no word of explanation, I was ordered home. And it looked like, if all went smoothly, that I would be there in early September.

It was a typical case of "hurry up and wait." By the time all the connections were made, I was at my wife's side only one day before she went into labor. She was thirty-five years old, and the labor was long and hard. The day passed, and the night, and still she labored. In those days, fathers weren't allowed in the delivery room, so I paced the streets drinking chocolate malts, one after another, praying for a safe birth.

At six o'clock the following morning, the doctor appeared in the waiting room. "It's a girl!" he said, "And she's healthy and strong."

I quickly made my way to the viewing window and looked at the babies, all lined up in a row. I knew my daughter immediately. She looked like me, and her mother, and my father, and a lot of other relatives, all rolled into one. She was beautiful.

When we finally took her home, I walked the floor with her, singing in my off-key voice about far-away places with strange sounding names. I bought her a music box that played "Anchors Aweigh." I told her stories about ships, and sailors, and seas and tides, and I told her about an answered prayer that brought me home from sea to be with my little girl.

G. J.,
San Diego, CA

Part 2

"*Walk beside the pony, Daddy; it's my first ride.*"
"*I know the cake looks funny, Daddy, but I
sure tried.*"

There's an amazing bond between dads and daughters. It
may be a powerful, almost painful, emotional link. Or it
may simply be a unique friendship built on mutual
respect and delight. As you'll discover in the following
Butterfly Kisses stories, when little girls try to please
their dads, they do it in the most creative ways. And
when dads try to please their daughters, the sky's the
limit. Whether all the effort is successful or not, the
result is still wonderful—fathers and daughters usually
manage to build a love connection that lasts for a lifetime.

*S*he was just eleven-months-old the day I took her for her first pony ride. A carnival had come to town, and as my wife took our picture, I walked around the circular track beside my smiling daughter. Her head was still bald like a baby's, but she was beginning to turn into a little girl. She was just learning to make her way around the living room, moving from tables to chairs to knees without falling down. She hadn't quite let go and tried to walk on her own, but it wouldn't be long. She was growing up.

The following afternoon I was left alone with my daughter while my wife worked. It was a hot and sticky day and my daughter was teething and fussy. I was exhausted—we'd been up with her several times the night before—and I stretched out on the couch and flipped on the TV. Both my daughter and I were cranky, and at that moment I wished I were anywhere but with her. As much as I hate to admit it, there were times back then when I wondered why God had given me a daughter instead of the son I'd always wanted.

All at once I heard a man singing, "Walk beside the pony, Daddy; it's my first ride." The song—"Butterfly Kisses"—went on to tell the story of a father and his daughter, and how quickly the little girl grew up and became a woman.

It was never my style to cry over songs, or for that matter, over anything else. But for me, this was more than a song. I began to sob. I realized that before long, my little girl would be walking around all by herself. Her bald head would be covered with thick, curly hair like her mother's. Her teeth would have grown into a beautiful smile. In an instant, I knew why God had given me a daughter. And I understood that He had given me far more than that. He'd given me a heart.

T. A.,
Stillwater, OK

33

I can't hear Christmas songs without thinking of my Dad. We've had a family tradition, for as long as I can remember, of gathering in my parents' den and listening to favorite holiday recordings. Dad has always collected Christmas albums, and besides his current CDs, he has a matchless collection of long play records that dates all the way back to the late sixties. He still plays them on the turntable he's had since I was a little girl.

Of course I remember the classics—the timeless carols, the majestic hymns like "O Holy Night," "Hark the Herald Angels Sing," and the "Hallelujah Chorus." I also recall the lighthearted sounds of "Rudolph the Red-nosed Reindeer," "Frosty the Snowman," and "Winter Wonderland." But my favorite memory carries me back to my earliest Christmases and a lovely song recorded by Jim

Reeves called "Snowflake." Every year, when Christmas rolled around, my Dad would hold me close to him as he danced around the room, his beautiful voice singing in my ear, "Hey, snowflake . . . my pretty little snowflake."

The smell of hot chocolate and cookies, the crackling fire and the music are like vivid snapshots that will always stay in my heart. Not long ago I reminded my Dad about "Snowflake" and our "dances" together. He was moved to tears, surprised and touched that I would remember something as long-ago as that. The truth is, my Dad is so much a part of my holiday memories that I can't imagine ever spending Christmas Eve anywhere but in the family den. I wish we could always be there together with the warm fire, the cookies and cocoa, and those wonderful records spinning around on the old turntable, filling the air with music—Dad's Christmas music.

D. D.,
Nashville, TN

*W*hen I was eleven, I decided to bake some cookies. My mother tried to help me, but I was an independent kid, and I more or less told her to get lost. I carefully measured the ingredients into the bowl, and mixed and poured and dropped them onto the cookie sheets with great enthusiasm.

When the first sheet was done, my older brothers came in and started eating them. Or, I should say, they tried to eat them. Those cookies were as hard as rocks. It was almost impossible to bite them. My brothers decided to use them as ammunition, throwing them at each other like miniature hand grenades. They only stopped their cookie war once or twice to make fun of me for being such an awful baker, and to point out that I was also ugly, stupid, and otherwise unlovable.

About that time, my dad came home from work.

Of course my brothers left the room quickly, but not before Daddy sized up the situation. "You made cookies?" he asked, smiling and ignoring my tear-stained face.

"Yeah, but they're not very good."

"Oh, I don't know about that."

Dad poured himself a cup of hot coffee, and proceeded to dunk the rock-hard cookies into it, softening them up enough to get them into his mouth. He ate so many that I was afraid he'd be sick. Then he gave me a big hug. "You're not only pretty," he said. "But you're a good cook, too."

He was so convincing that, to this day, I still think he meant every word of it.

L. P.,
Milton, PA

*W*hen I was in elementary school, my dad's company transferred him from the Midwest to California. I was really upset when I heard about the move. I had lots of friends, and saying goodbye to them was the saddest experience I'd ever had. Dad told me at the time how sorry he was for the upheaval in our lives, and I knew he was sincere. But I still felt terrible about it, and I guess he thought I was mad at him.

We arrived at our new home in August, and Dad took it upon himself to make sure I had some new friends. His first stop was at the school I would be attending. He made an appointment with the principal and asked her what kinds of activities would be available for girls my age once school started. She put in him in touch with Girl Scouts and a couple of other local clubs. While we were at church the next Sunday,

Dad talked to the youth pastor about choirs, sports, and other social opportunities. Over the next few weeks, Dad talked to several neighbors and even had a surprise swimming party for me at another family's pool.

By the time we'd been in town for a month, I was practicing with the church's children's choir, I had joined two girls' clubs and was attending church both Sunday and Wednesday nights. Once school started, I already knew several of the students in my class. In fact, I never really felt like a "new kid," because of all my dad did to help me.

As if that weren't enough, when it came time for our family vacation, he flew my best friend from "back home" out to be with me during our trip. My Dad knew how hard relocation can be on children, and he did everything in his power to help me adjust to our new home. It wasn't long before I liked California better than I'd ever liked the Midwest.

T. P.,

Ventura, CA

J've been a weekend fisherman all my life, so when my six-year-old daughter asked me if she could go fishing with me, I thought it might be fun. I'd decided to take her out to the beach, teach her how to bait a hook, and see how she liked it. I borrowed a fishing pole from my brother, and we headed out before dawn on a Saturday morning.

It was just getting light when we arrived at the beach. The tide was in, and the waves were large. I placed our lunch, our fishing gear, and our towels against a cliff, and took her with me to find some mussels for bait. We broke a couple of them open, and after she'd pricked her finger a few times and shed a few tears, she got pretty good at baiting hooks. We cast into the water and waited. I caught a couple of reasonably large fish, and she watched me reel them in. "Don't you think it hurts them when they get caught?" she asked.

"I don't think they know the difference," I consoled her. But she still looked a little worried as they flopped around in the bucket.

"Do you think we should throw them back?" she wondered aloud.

"How can we have them for dinner if we throw them back?" I said.

I tried to distract her by explaining what the pole would feel like if she got a bite, and pretty soon she told me to look—sure enough, her pole was bobbing up and down. She pulled and tugged, and eventually yelled for me to help her. Five minutes later I helped her reel in the biggest fish I'd ever seen anyone catch on those rocks. It must have weighed fifteen pounds, and it would have fed our entire family and the neighbors, too. I could almost see it sizzling on the barbecue.

But when I looked at my daughter, she was crying. "Daddy, it tried so hard to get away. It's not fair to kill it. We can buy fish at the store."

To make a long story short, we threw the big, beautiful fish back into the ocean. On the way home, we stopped at the fish market, and bought a replacement—already dead and filleted. And as we unloaded our gear from the car, my sweet and sensitive daughter told me that she thought it would be better if she didn't go fishing again. "Fishing makes me too sad," she concluded.

K. D.,

Birmingham, AL

*M*y daughter and I never really hit it off. I had three sons before she was born, and I never had a moment's difficulty relating to them. But my daughter was a challenge. For a long time, I really didn't think we liked each other, and I was deeply worried about our incompatibility. It made me feel guilty, like a failure. The older she got, the worse our relationship became. And I didn't have a clue what to do about it.

One day she came home from high school and announced that she needed a softball glove—she was going to play on the school team. I was completely taken off guard. I had never once imagined my daughter having any interest in sports, and I couldn't even conceive of her being athletically talented. But I had played softball for years, and I figured the least I could do was to buy her a glove.

We went to the sporting goods store and, as usual, we rode along in silence. Inside the store, I showed her the difference between one glove and another, bought a bottle of oil to soften the leather, and got her a ball and a bat. I noticed she was listening to me with unusual interest and that she hadn't argued with me even once.

When we got home, it was still light, and she asked me if I would play catch with her for a few minutes. Of course I did. To my surprise, she never missed a ball. I handed her the bat, and pitched a few balls to her. She knocked them halfway down the street. I looked at her, and she looked at me, and we both started laughing.

From that day on, my daughter and I were friends. Somehow, we bonded over a sport we both enjoyed and then found out how many other things we had in common. She's gone to college now, on a soft-ball scholarship. And she calls me after every game, tells me how she did, and asks my advice. She really

is a more talented athlete than her brothers or I. And
to be honest, I still can't believe it!

S. P.,
Jackson, TN

*P*eople thought I was a tomboy when I was little, but the truth was, I loved my Daddy so much that I wanted to be just like him. I thought my dad held the sun, the moon, and the stars in the palm of his hand. I tried to walk like him, talk like him, and I even tried to drive my three-wheeler the way he drove his car. He was a natural Mr. Fixit, and when he repaired something, I wanted him to show me how. If he could to do it, I wanted to be able to do it, too.

If Dad changed the oil in the car, I insisted that he show me how to change it, too. And he did. If he fixed the plumbing, I had to be taught how the wrench worked, how the water got shut off, and how a washer fit into a faucet. If Dad painted a room, I had to have my own paint roller and pan, and my own area to cover.

When I turned five, my mother went out and

bought me the most expensive birthday cake she could find. It was a beautiful pink color; it was covered in bright balloons made of icing, and it had my name in big purple letters. It was a masterpiece, and I wanted to carry it into the dining room myself. Mom let me try, but I tripped over my own feet and dropped the whole thing into one big, pink mess right in the middle of the kitchen floor.

Everybody at the party caught their breath. Mom screamed and I thought she was going to cry. "It's okay," I told her, patting her arm sympathetically. "Daddy's right here. And Daddy can fix it."

H. O.,
Waverly, IA

*W*hen I was seventeen and a senior in high school, my dad's company transferred him to a different state. It was a blow to our family. Although Dad wasn't one to say a lot about his feelings, he was always really good to me, and I knew being away from us was really hard on him.

On my eighteenth birthday, he was in New York. Although he tried to phone a couple of times, I never got the messages. It wasn't a particularly happy day for me because of some things that went wrong at school. But the worst of it was that Dad wasn't there on my birthday.

The next morning he called the house before I left for school. When he wished me a happy birthday and asked me how my day had gone, I started crying and couldn't stop. Finally I just told him, "I had a terrible day, and I wish you'd been here."

That afternoon, I was called out of class and asked to report to the school office. When I got there, I found that a dozen pink roses had been delivered to me. When I read the card, I started crying all over again. It said, "I love you. Dad."

Like I said before, Dad isn't one to express his feelings. But when he does, he means it. And on that day, I heard him loud and clear.

S. B.,
Atlanta, GA

$\mathcal{T}$alk about a generation gap! My dad is seventy-years-old and I'm twenty-two. But I don't think two people could be better friends than he and I.

My mom died when I was in kindergarten and Papa never remarried. I think my mother was the love of his life, and he just couldn't imagine finding someone to take her place. So it was just the two of us, and he and I were a pretty weird pair—the older guy with the little kid. Everybody always thought he was my grandpa.

Papa had to work hard at his job in road construction. I don't know where he found the energy, but he always had time to play games with me, to shop, go to the zoo, take vacations. We fished on the lake in the summers and through the ice in the winters. He tried to learn to ski with me, and he even figured out how to help me curl my hair for special occasions.

Papa was always there to help with my homework, to talk with me about boyfriend problems, and to explain a few other things that he probably never imagined he'd have to deal with! He was honest and kind, trying his best to see things from a "girl's" point of view.

I wanted a dog so much, and of course he knew that he really didn't have time to take care of one. But, as it turned out, the dog we got became Papa's best friend once I started going out. That was a relief to me, because I felt really torn about leaving him when I finally started working and dating.

I got married last year, and Papa was so proud to walk me down the aisle. My husband really under-stands that I need to live close to my father. I will take care of him until the day he dies, because as far as I can see, he's the best father on earth.

M. H.,
Little Rock, AK

Part 3

With all that I've done wrong,

I must have done something right . . .

∞

As fathers, we don't always live up to the gifts we've been given. Sometimes we stumble in little ways; sometimes we fall in big ways.

As you are about to see, we often receive letters which demonstrate how the love between fathers and daughters may be shaken or even shattered by the mistakes we make. Fortunately, where love thrives, grace lives.

*W*hen my wife and I were married just eleven months, we had our first baby. He was the son I had always dreamed of, and he was beautiful. He looked very much like my wife, and I was absolutely in awe of him. Maybe I loved him too much, I don't know. But when he was just eight-months-old, he died of S.I.D.S. (Sudden Infant Death Syndrome).

My world fell apart, and I started drinking too much. My wife and I separated two or three times, and then, while things seemed to be at their worst, she found out she was pregnant again.

At first I was devastated. How was I supposed to love another baby? I'd let myself fall in love with the last one, and I'd lost him. How could I let myself be that vulnerable ever again? I watched my wife's body changing and growing, and I felt more helpless every day.

The first few minutes after our daughter was born, I didn't want to hold her. But as I looked at her little face, I knew that I could not withhold my love from her just to protect myself. I started to cry in the delivery room. I prayed: "God, please don't take this one from me. I just can't go through that again."

To my amazement, I fell in love with my little girl just as I had done before with my son. Every day I thanked God for her life and prayed that I would be a good father. I got into an alcohol program so I wouldn't drink too much. And I learned to love my wife again, too. We became a truly happy family and put all our heartaches behind us.

When my daughter was twenty-one, she married a police officer. She was pregnant with their first child when her husband was killed in the line of duty. She came home to live with her mother and me, and a month later, she gave birth to her baby—a son who looked remarkably like our lost baby.

Our son-in-law's death, in some ways, was a

replay of our past tragedy. Once again, we found our-selves asking the "why?" questions, while realizing there were no easy answers. Little by little, however, my daughter learned to laugh again. We all have.

Today, after all the pain, we've learned to count our blessings. As for me, I am truly grateful. My lovely daughter is still close by, and in my grandson, I have the little boy I always dreamed of. For the second time in my life, my daughter has given me a wonder-ful gift of life and love.

D. D.,

Alexandria, VA

*W*hen people talk about their fathers, I have to ask them to make an exception on my part. The only dad I ever really had was my grandfather. My father abandoned our family when I was just a baby. My mother had to work to support us, so Grandpa stepped in and took over. He is loving; he is understanding; he is cheerful. Above all else, Grandpa loves my brother, sister, and me as if we were his own kids.

One of the things I love most about my grandpa is his availability. No matter what my need is, day or night, weekday or weekend, he never fails to stop everything to listen. He turns off the television, puts down the newspaper, set his tools aside—whatever he is doing takes second place to me. And I'm not the only one he treats that way. Friends, family, even strangers always have his full attention. People come first for him; he puts them and their concerns above his own.

Grandpa often says, "Well, you know I've got no problems of my own, so I've got lots of time for yours." The reality is somewhat different. He has all sorts of health problems, and in fact he rarely has a day that is completely pain free. Yet his personal comfort never seems to cross his mind. His favorite question is "What can I do to help?" And his most frequent conclusion is, "Well, we'll just pray about it and see what God does."

Grandpa is everything I need to show me what a real dad is supposed to be like.

E. J.,
Jacksonville, FL

*M*y dad's words are burned forever in my memory. "Honey, this is hard, but I've got to tell you something. I'm a homosexual." Suddenly, everything I'd believed in collapsed around me. My innocent view of my father, my family, and my life was shattered.

Of course the first question that came to my mind was obvious, "How can you be gay and be a father? You've been married to Mom for twenty years—how come you didn't know about this before? Are you sure?"

Later, many of my questions had to do with me. What would my friends think if they found out? What would happen if my Dad and I went out in public together? The worst question of all came up when I started remembering the way things were between him and me in my childhood—his goodnight hugs, the times he'd been so warm and sweet. If he hadn't loved my mother, had he ever really loved me?

At first I was so angry that I never wanted to see him again. When he suggested that I meet his "partner" I screamed horrible things at him and even tried to hit him. He was gone for several months after that. I guess the break was good, because it gave me time to think and sort things out in my mind.

Mom insisted that all of us see a counselor, and looking back I know she was right. At the time, however, I didn't want anybody's help or anybody's opinion. I just wanted to be angry and to punish my father for what he'd done. It took more than a year for me to get that out of my system.

Now, Dad and I are starting to be friends again. I have a hard time trusting him the way I used to. Because he hid his secret life from me before, I can't believe him anymore the way he'd like me to. But little by little I'm learning to love him again. I don't like to think about his lifestyle. But I don't want to lose him forever, either.

If one good thing has come out of all this it's that I think it's made me a more caring person. It's taught me that people everywhere have to deal with all kinds of pain, and a lot of times, that pain is hidden.

L. V.,
Bloomington, IN

*O*ne day I was listening to the radio, and I heard the "Butterfly Kisses" song. Like most people, I cried when I heard it. But I didn't cry because my father loved me. I cried because he was so abusive, and because he would never be the father I'd always longed to have.

When my Mom listened to the song with me, she cried too. She told me she was sorry that I hadn't experienced a father's love. I think she blamed herself for a lot of the things that went wrong in our family, and that was so unfair.

"Mom," I told her, "I'm not sad because I've never felt the love of a father. I'm just thankful for you. You've been both a mother and a father to me. You should get twice as many *Butterfly Kisses* as other moms."

Fortunately, I met a wonderful man who is nothing at all like my father. When we were planning our wedding, I thought about the song and about my mother. I asked our pastor if it would be all right with him if Mom gave me away. He told me it was the nicest idea he'd ever heard.

When the wedding march started to play, I put my arm through mom's arm, and she walked down the aisle with me. She looked so beautiful and so happy. And when our pastor asked "Who gives this woman to be married to this man . . . ?" my mother proudly said, "I do."

My mother had to fill my unloving father's shoes in almost every way. Most of all she loved me enough for two people. I can never thank her enough.

J. B.,
Charleston, SC

*W*hen I was a tiny girl, I loved my father very much. But as years went by, I learned that to love Dad was to love two different people. One of them was a funny and entertaining character that everybody loved. The other was a drunk who beat up my mother. As I grew into a young woman's body, that wasn't all he did when he'd been drinking. On at least three occasions he came into my room, crawled into my bed, and sexually molested me.

Of course I was terrified. I hated the sound of the door closing behind him when he came home from the bar late at night. I hated the sound of his voice and the smell of his breath. I tried to get my brother to stay in the room with me, but I didn't dare tell him why, so he always left when he got sleepy. I was afraid to tell my mother what had happened—I knew if she confronted my father, there would be terrible trouble. Violence was a very real possibility, and in my worst moments, I wondered if he would kill her.

Even after I grew up and left home, my father's visits to my room haunted me. After a couple of failed marriages, I began to seek help for the heavy drinking problem I had developed. In the course of my quest for healing, I became a Christian believer and was faced with a completely new spiritual concept: forgiveness.

How could I forgive my father? And yet it was clearly part of the package—if God was going to forgive me, I needed to forgive those who had "trespassed" against me. "Lord," I prayed, "I don't know how to do this, but I want to do what's right. So please help me."

Things didn't change overnight, but eventually there was a difference in my attitude. Little by little, I began to see my father through new eyes. By now he was an old, sick man who no longer drank. I was able to laugh at his jokes—he really was very funny. I was able to reminisce with him about good times we'd had together as a family–and there had been some great times. Gradually, I was able to appreciate the good side of my father and to simply set the rest aside. He never asked me to forgive him, maybe because he didn't remember what had happened while he was drunk. And I chose not to confront him. But God asked me to forgive him, and so I did. And when my father died, I cried in genuine grief. To my surprise, I had learned to love him.

J. R.,
Canton, OH

I was just sixteen when I found out that my girlfriend Madelaine was pregnant, and by the time I heard about it, she had already left town to have the baby someplace faraway. My parents were furious at everybody—her, me, her parents, even the school. And they refused to let me contact her or her family. I wasn't even allowed to say I was sorry, or to try to help. "She's a cheap girl and she got herself pregnant," they said. "You stay away from her, and that's final."

Madelaine moved to a different state, and I heard two years later that she'd had a baby girl and had refused to put her up for adoption. The girl's name was Judy—after Judy Collins, whose music we had both loved. Every time I thought about that little girl, I felt torn up inside. I wondered what kind of personality she had, whether she was anything like me, and whether she looked like Madelaine. Young as I was, I had really loved Madelaine, and as much as I tried not to think about the whole situation, I never quite succeeded. Sometimes I prayed that God would let me see them again. Most of the time, I just wondered what had happened. Fourteen years went by.

By then I was living and working in New York—three states away from our hometown. One afternoon I was walking down a sidewalk, and I noticed a woman in a parked car. I did a double take, unable to believe my eyes. It was Madelaine. Or at least it looked exactly like her. I broke out into a sweat, and my hands started shaking. I tapped on the car window. She looked up at me and her face went white with shock.

"I've been looking for you for years," I told her. "I want to see my daughter. I've wanted to help out with child support, or do whatever I could, but no one knew where you were."

Madelaine was cold at first. She had become very

embittered toward my family and me, and I could see why. I asked her to forgive me and said I would try to make it up to her. We talked for a while, and I learned that she was recently divorced from her husband. I had just been through a divorce, too. She also told me that she was parked there waiting for Judy to finish a dance lesson. "She'll be out here in a few minutes."

When Judy showed up, I was stunned. She looked so much like me that I couldn't believe my eyes. The only difference was—she was beautiful. She looked at me without interest, and when Madelaine explained to her who I was, she stared at me as if I were from another planet.

For the next year, I visited once a week and gave them money every month. It wasn't easy trying to build a relationship with either one of them. But, little by little, the ice thawed. Once Judy and I got better acquainted, it was obvious that we were uncannily alike—not just in appearance, but in likes and dislikes, moods, and every other way you could imagine.

And as for Madelaine, she must have been the best single mom on earth. She had somehow managed to put Judy into an excellent private school and had provided her with everything she could possibly afford. And she had worked two jobs to do it. I was amazed at her resourcefulness and her devotion to her daughter—our daughter.

Madelaine and I began to see each other without Judy. We were both extremely self-protective, and I'm really amazed that we ever managed to work things out. The hardest part for Madelaine was the first trip we made to visit my parents. But we all learned some lessons about forgiving and starting over. Madelaine and I were married when Judy was seventeen, and the three of us really are "one big happy family." It will always be a miracle for me to sit with the love of my life and watch our daughter grow into a beautiful young woman.

R. S.,
New York, NY

$\mathcal{F}$or most of my forty years I have longed for the kind of "dad" I never had. I wanted a dad who was responsible, kind, loving, and respectable. As long as I could remember, my father's alcoholism never left room in his life for anything else. The bottle came first, and if he ever got sober, everyone was so mad at him that he might as well have stayed drunk.

In the last year, I've witnessed the most amazing miracle of my life. It started out in the worst way—my dad was found unconscious in the street, and the police took him to the hospital, where he nearly died. It wasn't the first time he'd passed out, but by now his age was catching up with him and his health was at risk.

Mom and I dutifully went to visit him, going through motions of being "family" the way we'd always done. When we got to his room, we found the hospital chaplain at his bedside, and they seemed to be having a rather serious conversation. Never before had I seen my father cry when he was sober. My mother and I gave each other a look and said we'd wait outside.

A few minutes later, the chaplain came out and got us. "He has some things he'd like to say to you," he told us as he left. More curious than ever, we went into the room.

Dad stared at us for a minute, obviously searching for the right words. Finally he began, "I have given my life to Jesus Christ," he said. "I've asked him to forgive my sins against him and my sins against you. I want you to forgive me, if you possibly can, and I want to start my life over."

From that day on, our lives were never the same. Dad faithfully attended A.A. meetings, went to church three times a week, and did everything he could to be a part of the family. Six months later, the miracle was repeated in the life of my older brother, who also became a Christian and stopped drinking.

I thought I knew both those men very well. But in fact, I'm just getting acquainted with them now. All the good things about them that were hidden in the alcoholic fog have begun to shine in their personalities like gold. My father is a delightful person, and he and I have learned to love each other deeply. I wouldn't have believed it was possible, yet it has really happened.

For the first time in my life, I have the Dad I always wanted. I used to wonder why my mother didn't divorce him and get on with her life. Now I understand. She knew that a good man lived inside that broken shell, and she had enough faith to believe that God would someday release him and renew him. It seems too good to be true, but that's exactly what happened.

A. J.,
Chattanooga, TN

Part 4

One part woman, the other part girl.

To perfume and makeup from ribbons and curls

❧

One of the greatest challenges fathers and daughters
face is the time when little tiny girls begin to trans-
form into mature and attractive young women.
Daughters find themselves caught between two
worlds—girlhood and womanhood. Dads find themselves watching a butterfly emerge from a cocoon, and
once the process begins, there is no turning back. The
Butterfly Kisses stories we've been told about those
in-between years describe both fathers and daughters
who have put their relationship with each other above

all complications: their fears, their misunderstandings, their disappointments, their uncertainties, and—at times—their heartfelt sadness.

*M*y wife and I have always tried to keep the communication open between our daughters and ourselves. At times it has meant swallowing our fears, our opinions, and our criticism and just listening. That isn't easy, when you see your kids on the verge of making huge mistakes, and sometimes we've jumped in and given them our best advice when we thought it was really necessary. But a lot of times, especially as they've gotten older, we've just learned to listen and pray, and hope they'll make the right decisions.

The summer before our oldest daughter left for college, she was struggling through a lot of emotional issues. Her girlfriends were leaving, one by one, for universities across the country. The farewell parties were starting to feel like wakes, and her uneasiness grew worse because she knew she needed to break up with her boyfriend, and she just couldn't quite bring herself to do it.

One night my wife and I were lying in bed when she tiptoed to the door. "Can I come in?" she whispered.

"Are you okay?"

"Not really . . ."

She sat on the side of the bed for a minute, and then she stretched out in the middle between us, like she'd done a thousand times as a little girl. "Can I just talk?" she asked. "I already know the answers, but I just need to talk . . ."

For the next hour she poured out her heart. And as she did, I thought to myself that it was a wonderful compliment to us that, at her age, she still wanted to talk to us. It wasn't our advice she wanted. More than anything else, she simply needed our presence, our unspoken concern, and our unconditional love.

J. M.,
Santa Barbara, CA

*M*y dad was a farmer, and he didn't know much about "the women." He was kind to my mother, and he never raised his voice in our home. But he kept his distance from situations that required him to interact with females. Even when I tried to start conversations with him, I could see that he felt a little uncomfortable, and our dialogue never lasted long.

That is why, looking back, one thing my father always did seems completely out of character. I was a ballet student from first grade through high school, and every year the local dance studio held a large dance recital. We performed for several days in a row, and all the local communities attended. Every year, on open-ing night, my father gave me a bottle of perfume. When I was little, it was always a floral scent. But as I got

79

older, he bought me real perfumes from the department store.

Every year, the ritual was the same. We'd get dressed, mom would take my picture, and then dad would appear with a small, gift-wrapped present. I'd open it and put some behind my ears on my neck. I would thank him and ask, "Does it smell good, Daddy?" He would smile and nod. I'd kiss him on the cheek, thank him again, and we'd get in the car and drive to the performance.

C. W.,
Charlotte, NC

$\mathcal{J}$’ve heard it said that trouble brings people together. But it wasn’t true of my father and me. When Mom died, my father and I grew apart. I was in my early teens, and now Dad says he didn’t know what to do with me. But I think the real reason is that he was afraid to love again.

Dad and I are more alike than either of us wants to admit. And I think he and I both went through the same kind of sadness, remorse, and sorrow. Mom was the kind of person who never demanded anything from the people who loved her. It was too easy to take her for granted. And, once she was gone, it was impossible to replace her.

A couple of years ago, I decided that it was up to me to rebuild my relationship with Dad. I tried to imag-ine what Mom would do under the same circumstances, and before long, I had an idea. On Father's Day, I informed him that I was taking him out to his favorite restaurant. I made reservations, and soon we were seated at a beautiful table overlooking the river. While we were waiting for our food, I told Dad that I understood how hard it was for him to love me. I'd done a lot of things that upset him. But I apologized for my faults and told him that I hoped he would forgive me and try to love me anyway.

He couldn't have looked more shocked. "But I do love you!" He was defensive at first, but as we talked about it, I helped him understand that even if he felt love for me on the inside, he wasn't letting me see it on the outside. He explained that he's not a demonstrative person, but promised that he would try harder anyway.

A few days later, I found a beautiful card on the dining room table. Written inside was a message from my Dad. "Thanks for loving me enough to reach out to me. I'm sorry you thought I didn't love you, because I do. I'm ready to stop grieving and start living again, and I hope we can enjoy each other more now. Your loving father."

> B. J.,
> Culpepper, VA

*H*ow can a mother pack up and leave four children? I'm a mother myself now, and I'll never understand it. But that's what my mother did. When I was five years old, she drove off in the family car one day and she never came back. My father was left to raise us all.

Dad worked two jobs so he'd have enough money to provide for us, and somehow he still found the time to have fun with us. He took us fishing and camping. We went to carnivals, zoos, and to movies. Never once did we feel neglected or alone. And most amazing of all, he never said a bad word about our mother. He never judged her, and he never judged us. He just reminded us that we were to love and forgive her, and that's all he had to say.

When I was twelve, Dad decided I needed to

84

learn the facts of life. He was so embarrassed that he could hardly explain what he was trying to say, and eventually he asked my older sister to come in and help him. But he knew it was his responsibility, so he took it. Not long thereafter, it became pretty obvious that I needed to wear a bra. Daddy drove me to Sears and helped me find the size I needed.

Being a single father must be one of the most difficult jobs in the world. But Daddy never made it seem difficult at all. I think, in many ways, he enjoyed it. He's now in his eighties, and all four of us are having the time of our lives spoiling him and making sure he has everything he needs. It's the very least we can do.

G. K.,
Louisville, KY

85

*A*fter my remarriage, I became very concerned about my sixteen-year-old daughter. Amanda is a sweet, open young girl with a wonderful personality and a beautiful appearance. At the time, she was still living with her mother, and her mother had a lot of boyfriends over—many times they would spend the night. The example she was setting for Amanda wasn't the greatest, but I didn't know what to say or how to broach the subject.

One weekend Amanda stayed with us, and while she was out with some friends, my new wife came to me with a look of great concern on her face. "I hate to tell you this, but I just went into the guest room, and Amanda had left this—open—on the bed."

My wife handed me a diary, and the pages were filled with explicit details about Amanda's intimate relationships with three different boys. I was sickened and angry as I read it. I wanted to blame somebody for this awful situation. I started with my ex-wife, but before long I was blaming both Amanda and myself just as much. I didn't know what to do or where to turn. I was just about to get in the car to go find Amanda and confront her when my wife sat down with me and asked me to listen to her.

"Don't you understand?" she said. "She's asking for help. Why else would she leave it out in plain view? She wanted us to find it. She knows she's in trouble, and she left her diary open so somebody would read it. Don't be too hard on her. Let's try to get her to talk to us, and maybe we can really do something positive for her. I don't blame you for being angry, but I don't think your anger is going to solve anything."

I knew she was right. I did my best to calm down, and by the time Amanda got home, I was ready to talk to her in a self-controlled and even loving way.

I showed her the diary, and she immediately started to cry. "I'm sorry . . ." she said.

All my carefully rehearsed lines were forgotten. I put my arms around her and said, "Amanda, we love you so much. What can we do to help?"

From that moment on, things began to change. Within two months, we were awarded custody, and Amanda was living with us. She changed schools, made new friends, started seeing a counselor, and began going to church with us.

Little by little, we learned just how much the divorce had wounded her and how her mother's behavior had upset her. But the biggest lesson she learned, she told me, was the one that meant the most to me: "I never realized before," she told me, "just how much I needed my Dad."

A. H.,
Merrill, WI

$\mathcal{D}$ad was always good to me. I can think of a million little things that he did to let me know he loved me. He sat through my dance recitals. He coached my (awful) baseball team. He ate my cooking and baking experiments as if they were gourmet treats, when no one else could stomach them.

But there were a couple of things he did that weren't so little. When I was in high school I went through my first "love" experience, and it ended badly. After my boyfriend broke up with me so he could go out with my close friend, I cried for hours and hours. I couldn't stop. I just closed the door to my room and sobbed my heart out.

Dad came into my room at ten-thirty, then at eleven, and once more at midnight to check on me. Finally he dragged in a down comforter and a pillow, and slept on the floor next to me. He didn't say anything about it, and I remember waking up in the night and hearing him snoring. The next morning, before he left for work, he got a cold washcloth and put it on my eyes so they wouldn't look so puffy and red.

A few years later, after I got married, I had a miscarriage. After work Dad stopped by to see me. He didn't say much—he just sat on the bed and held my hand. When I looked at him, he had tears in his eyes.

I don't think I've ever heard my Dad actually say, "I love you." But he's said it in so many ways that there's no question about it in my mind.

P. D.,
Springfield, MO

$\mathcal{D}$ad and I started "dating" when I was ten years old. At first we were both kind of embarrassed, but mom explained that it was a chance for us to go out and get to know each other better. And Dad explained that if I got used to being treated nicely by him, I wouldn't settle for less from other men.

So every couple of weeks, I would take a bubble bath, wash and curl my hair, and put one of my prettiest dresses. Mom would help me, and when I got all ready, Dad would be waiting for me in the living room. He always brought me a single pink rose, and I'd put it in a vase before we went out.

Dad would take me out to eat and then to a movie, a music recital, or a play at the school. Sometimes there would be a concert at our church, or some other event that he thought I would enjoy. But the best part, at least for me, was the time we spent talking. I think we got to know each other better during our "dates" than we could have ever done if we'd just stayed home and had some informal conversation.

And Dad was right—when I started dating boys my own age, I always compared them to Dad. I didn't expect every one of them to bring me a rose, or to be sophisticated and mature, but I knew from experience how it felt to be treasured. And when I finally met the wonderful man who was to become my husband, one of the first things I noticed was that he always brought me flowers. And the most important thing between us was the conversation we shared—from our first date till today, he's always enjoyed talking to me, and I still love talking to him.

B. T.,
Cincinnati, OH

*A*s long as my dad was around, I always felt safe. He was like a big, protective wall against the outside world. He and I were able to talk about everything, and I really trusted his opinion and his beliefs. When I got old enough to learn about the birds and the bees, I learned them from Dad. He may not have had the most polished approach to the subject, but he gave it to me straight.

My first boyfriend was the love of my life. I was so crazy about him that I could hardly think about any-thing else. But there was a problem—he wanted me to have sex with him, and I didn't think it was right. Dad had talked to me about all that, and I knew right from wrong. But my boyfriend was very persuasive, and I was afraid. I didn't want to lose him, but I didn't want to make a mistake, either.

Since Dad had always been my refuge, I did something that made great sense to me: I asked Dad to talk to my boyfriend about why I wouldn't have sex with him. Now in retrospect, I realize that this was a rather strange move on my part. At the outset, most Dads would have picked the boyfriend up and thrown him out of the house. And, even if the conversation had taken place, most boyfriends would have politely listened and immediately disappeared into thin air.

But my Dad is one in a million. He sat down with my boyfriend and told him how much he liked him and how welcome he was in our home. He let him know that I thought he was the greatest boyfriend in the world and that I was really happy with him. Then he went on to explain that we were a Christian family and that there were some values that were very important in our family. One of them was chastity. He gently and kindly informed my amorous beau that there were very few reasons that he wouldn't be invited back to our home; however, a continued effort at seducing me would qualify as one of the primary ones. And, when he was finished, he shook my dumbfounded boyfriend's hand and thanked him very much for listening.

Believe it or not, it worked. After that, my boyfriend and I continued to go out together for more than a year. And never again did he attempt to carry our physical relationship beyond the boundaries I had established. Maybe he was a little bit afraid of my Dad, but mostly, I think he respected him. In fact, I know he did. And as for me, nothing could have made me feel safer or more protected than my father's strong and wise intervention on my behalf.

S. W.,
Spring Hill, TN

Part 5

She asked me what I'm thinking and I said,

"I'm not sure,

I just feel like I'm losing my baby girl."

Every father knows that someday his daughter is going to leave, but there's rarely a time when he's really ready to say goodbye. Sometimes the reason for leaving is a wedding day, and my song "Butterfly Kisses" describes a loving dad's feelings about that event. Sometimes girls pack up and leave for college, preparing themselves for new responsibilities and challenges. Sometimes daughters leave in the midst of tears and unhappiness, moving on because of trouble or divorce. No matter why they leave us, dads feel the loss of their daughters more acutely than anyone knows. And daughters are forever torn between tomorrow and yesterday—between being daddy's little girl and being a grown-up woman facing the future on her own.

Our family was never one to say "I love you." There were four of us kids and not much communication between us and our rather old and "old fashioned" parents. My oldest sister was always one to get into trouble at school and was quick to tell Mom and Dad how much she disliked them. My brother disappeared into the gay community some time ago, and he doesn't keep in touch with us. My second sister died two years ago of Cystic Fibrosis. Now I'm the only one left at home.

My father isn't much of a talker. He keeps his thoughts to himself, and if he's not sure what to say he doesn't say anything. Not long ago, I came home with my boyfriend Jim, who wanted to ask Dad for my hand in marriage. The two of them went outside on the porch to talk, and when they came back in, my father's eyes were red, and his face was wet with tears.

"Daddy," I said, shocked by the sight of him, "Aren't you happy for us? Why are you crying?"

He just shook his head, pulled out his handkerchief and blew his nose.

"Daddy, what's wrong?" I went over to him and put my hands on his arms.

"Nothing's wrong," he murmured.

"Then why are you crying?"

He stood and looked at me for a minute and shook his head again. Finally Jim quietly suggested, "Why don't you tell her what you just told me?"

Dad nodded, took a deep breath and began the longest speech I've ever heard him make. "I told Jim that I'm happy enough for you to be marrying him. He's a good boy, and he'll be a good provider. But I want you to know that letting you go is the hardest thing I've ever done. You're the only one of the children that's ever asked if you could go. The others all left without caring what I thought or felt. And now you want to know if you can leave me, too."

"Daddy, I'm sorry . . ."

"Don't be sorry. The answer is yes. Of course you can marry Jim."

"We plan to stay close by, you know."

"I know," Dad nodded. He blew his nose again and left the room. In that one conversation, he'd told me more about himself, his hurts, and his heart than I'd ever imagined hearing. Most of all, I learned how much he loved me.

L. B.,

Raleigh, NC

101

*D*uring the last few days of my wedding preparations, I was spending less and less time with my parents. They didn't complain, but I felt guilty. I have always been "Papa's girl," and deep inside I was afraid that Papa was feeling hurt and rejected, even though he never said a word about it.

My father is a strong Latino man who doesn't express his gentle side very often. Of course we all know how soft his heart is, but he hides his feelings as carefully as possible. After the wedding rehearsal dinner, my fiancé and I went out for coffee by our-selves. As I was driving home, I heard "Butterfly Kisses" on the radio. I really started crying, because I knew, even though he would never say so, that it described my father's feelings perfectly.

I guess Dad didn't hear the car when I got back, because when I walked into the house, I found him looking at my baby pictures. He was crying. I rushed over and gave my sweet old Papa a huge hug. I'd never seen him cry before. That night we had the best conversation we'd ever had. We reminisced about all the good times we'd shared together. And to my surprise, Papa told me that he was scared of the thought that he might not see me anymore at our house. "Who will I play chess with?" he asked me, with a very solemn look on his face.

I promised that I would always visit him, and that we would still be a happy family—just a bigger one. Finally, with a hug, he told me to go to bed. "You need to get a good night's sleep."

"Goodnight, Papa," I smiled, wishing we could talk all night.

"Tomorrow's your big day," he said with a wink and his usual tough-guy grin. "And I want my daughter to look beautiful!"

J. P.,
Kissimmee, FL

Poem for a Runaway

You have been gone for more than a year;

Where are you, my daughter?

All by myself, under the roof, waiting, hoping.

Your mother's passed away,

And I wasn't even there to say goodbye.

I've lost one part of my life;

I can't lose you too.

Please come back.

Drugs and alcohol will kill you.

You're only sixteen

And you're the brightest part of my life.

Please forgive me.

Please come back to me.

No matter what you've done, I don't mind.

Anonymous

$\mathcal{G}$rowing up with a single dad seemed perfectly normal to me. My childhood and teenage years with Dad never seemed unusual or special until I went away to college and started missing him so much. When I talked to my roommate about him, and the way he'd always taken care of me, I began to realize how wonderful and unique my dad had always been.

My high school memories of Dad had to do with talks about the future, with plans for going away to school, with confidences about boys I liked and the dances I wanted them to take me to. Of course Dad thought I was the most beautiful girl in the world, and he had nothing good to say about the boys who didn't share his opinion.

But it was the childhood memories that really made me want to cry. I remembered Dad painstakingly brushing my long hair, being extra careful so it wouldn't hurt. I remembered him figuring out how to braid it and how to put it into a ponytail. Dad was a blue-collar kind of guy, and hairstyling wasn't exactly his best talent, but he tried so hard to make me "pretty as a picture."

Sometimes in the dorm I would lie awake at night, worrying about grades or exams or something else. That's when I would remember the lullabies Dad made up for me. The rhymes weren't exact, and his voice wasn't the greatest. But they were the sweetest songs in the world to me, because the words "I love you" were written between every line.

B. R.,
Horse Cave, KY

*T*here are two days in my daughter's life I will always remember. The first was the day of her birth, when her mother, the doctor, and I shared the experience of watching her come into the world. The hard work of delivery, the bright, sterile room, the fears of the unknown were all swept away by the sight of a beautiful baby girl. Holding her that day, so healthy and pink with life, remains in my memory as a miracle.

This was not just any baby girl—she was the one I had prayed for. We already had two sons, and now God had given us a daughter. It is difficult to describe in words the feelings I had as I held her, looked into her tiny face, and realized that she was here, she was ours, and she was perfect. My heart felt as if it would burst. She was to be our last child, the "baby" of the family.

There is another day that also remains in my mind, and I would say that it was far and away the most difficult day of my entire life. After talking to my sons a few hours before, I had to sit down with my precious, innocent eleven-year-old daughter and tell her that I was moving away. As much as I adored her, as dear to my heart as she and her brothers were to me, we would no longer be living in the same house. We would no longer be together as a family.

Her mother and I were getting a divorce.

In the months and years that have followed, I have never quite adjusted to our new way of life. I have tried very hard to assure my little girl—now she's a teenager—that I will always love her, and that I will always be here for her. But somehow, in spite of everything, a terrible pain remains in my heart. Sometimes at night I lie in my bed crying, missing my daughter and wishing I could still tuck her in bed at night.

I hope somehow, some way, she really knows

how much I love her. I hope I've managed to communicate that much to her. No matter what the circumstances she has been forced to live with, she will always be Daddy's little girl. I will always adore her.

C. F.,
Portland, TN

Part 6

I couldn't ask God for more, man, this is what
love is.
I know I've gotta let her go, but I'll always
remember . . .

☙

One of the most precious presents fathers and
daughters give each other is memories. The love we
share with one another never fades, and even after
we've said goodbye, we still have a collection of
mental snapshots that will stay with us for the rest of
our lives. As the *Butterfly Kisses* letters came in, one
of the themes that recurred was the loss of a father or
a daughter through death. Although there was great

sorrow in those stories, there was also a beautiful sense of remembrance and gratitude that seemed to somehow make the loss of a loved one a little easier to bear.

*W*hen we first found out that Megan was sick, it seemed like a bad dream. We somehow imagined that we would wake up some morning, and everything would be okay again. Megan would be tearing around the house in her pajamas, bouncing on our bed and waking us up. Her hair would be long and golden again, and her eyes would sparkle. That's what we kept thinking. And there were times of remission, when it seemed like our dreams would come true. But, eventually, we always found ourselves back at the hospital.

Taking Megan to her radiation treatments was unbearable for my wife, and deep inside I wanted to be the one there anyway. So we'd get up early, and I'd take her for her treatments and then drop her off at school. I was exhausted by this routine, both physically and emotionally. But when I thought about what this little seven-year-old girl was going through, I decided my tiredness really wasn't all that important.

For a while, during second grade Megan seemed to be making huge improvements. Again, our hopes soared. But then one day a call came from the school nurse: "Pick her up early, she's not doing well at all."

As I drove Megan to the hospital, she lost consciousness. From that episode on, she was paralyzed. There wasn't much anyone could do for her, but it made me feel better to rub her arms and legs with lotion. She smiled at me when I did it, and I knew she felt my love, even though she was so terribly sick. I'd sit and look at her and think that I couldn't love anyone more than I loved her. And yet we were going to lose her—there was little doubt in our minds.

The day Megan died it felt like something died in me, too. I believe in heaven, and I believe that Jesus will take me there someday. And the first person I'll see is Megan—she'll be healthy again. Her hair will be long and golden. And her eyes will sparkle, just like they used to.

S. P.,
Adrian, MI

*M*emories of my dad will always be bittersweet. He was such a wonderful father, and I can't think of a single time he didn't treat me like the "little princess" that he always said I was.

There were seven of us kids, and I was the youngest girl. By the time I started school, Dad had retired from his job, so I always got special treatment. If he was making snacks, he made my "special requests," even if he had to go to the store in order to do it. He would buy me candy bars at the store and put them in my room to surprise me. He'd hide little notes with silly pictures on them in my homework or my school lunch.

One morning when I was in the fourth grade, I hugged and kissed my dad, told him I loved him, and headed for the school bus. Later that morning, my teacher asked me to come outside and talk to her. I was surprised to see my uncle there, and he looked sad and worried. He told me we were going to pick up my brother and sister at middle school. By the time the four of us got home, Dad was dead.

They say children sometimes feel anger toward their deceased parents, or that they blame themselves for the parents' death. In my case, I felt nothing but sadness at the loss of a dear and loving friend. And when I say I have bittersweet memories, it's only because he was so sweet, and the loss of him was so bitter.

A. H.,
Colman, TX

*M*y father was middle-aged when I was born, and I don't think he knew much about being a dad. He didn't have much to say to me when I was a little girl, and he seemed shy when I tried to talk to him. But he never hesitated to give his "little Dolly" a big hug. And somewhere along the way, he picked up the idea of brushing his eyelashes against my face when he told me goodnight. I didn't know at the time that people called those little brushes "butterfly kisses."

I planned to get married on my parents' golden wedding anniversary. They loved the idea of a double celebration, and we all looked forward to the day with great excitement. When we were choosing the music for the reception, someone told me about the song "Butterfly Kisses." By then I knew that the song beautifully described the sweet, affectionate "kisses" my father had given me as a little girl.

When I had the lyrics to the song, I called my father on the phone and read the words to him. We had a wonderful conversation—one of the best of our lives—sharing memories of the past, and talking about the future. And when I danced with my father at the wedding, we danced to the song that had somehow captured the gentle love that had always been shared between us.

Two days after the wedding, my husband and I received word that my father had suddenly and unexpectedly died. For our rather reserved family, the wedding, the music, and the conversations that followed opened a floodgate of feelings. The words to a popular song had helped us understand and identify the love that ran deeply and quietly beneath the surface of our family life. I am so grateful, because it brought the love between my father out into the open, where I could see it and appreciate it.

T. M.,
Bell Buckle, TN

$\mathcal{D}$addy was eighty-six years old. He'd been battling cancer for a while, and I'd heard that he was getting weaker and weaker. So I called my uncle, who lived near him, and asked him to see how bad things really were. Uncle Otis wasn't in the greatest shape himself, but he promised to drive over and see what was happening.

He phoned me later that night. "I know you can't keep flying back and forth," my uncle reported, "but if I were you, I'd get up here as quick as you can. It's more important for you to see him alive than dead. And I don't think he's been able to eat or drink anything for more than a week."

If Daddy wasn't eating, he was very sick indeed. Food was his favorite subject. I felt so sad—my father and I had been the dearest of friends as long as I could remember. Never a day passed that I didn't think of some proverb he'd repeated a thousand times, or a valuable lesson he'd taught me, or some silly joke he'd completely worn out in the re-telling.

Daddy was a dear and wonderful man, and in his loneliness after my mother's death, he'd longed to share his life with someone. After all, he reminded me, they'd been married fifty-two years, and living alone didn't sound all that appealing. Although the woman he married was good to him, she had never accepted me. I was both hurt and quietly resentful. However, since she provided him with the companionship he craved, and seemed to be genuinely fond of him, I had no choice but to let him go.

Daddy and I had a more or less tacit understanding that his marriage needed to be his first priority. I would therefore keep a low profile. I only spoke to him on the phone when his wife wasn't home, and otherwise I stayed out of the way. He knew I loved him, and I knew he loved me, and for the past ten years that had been enough. But now that he was so sick, I would simply have to override his wife's disapproval and spend some final hours with him. I called the airlines and booked myself out on the first flight the next morning.

I arrived in his city mid-afternoon and took a cab directly to the hospital. My mind was filled with horrible images. How emaciated was he? How senile had he become? Was he conscious or unconscious by now? My uncle's report had been completely negative, so I tried to brace myself for the worst, whatever the worst might be.

I walked in the room, and when he saw me, Daddy smiled broadly and extended his arms. He was thin, a little yellowish, and he badly needed a shave. But I gave him a hug, and his eyes lit up with pleasure. My stepmother rushed out, explaining that she would try to find a chair for me. I sat down on the edge of the bed in the meantime, and Daddy and I started talking, laughing, and remembering.

I kept thinking that he didn't really look all that bad. How could my uncle have thought he was dying? I tried to get a handle on his condition, but he just laughed off my concern. "At my age, everything is terminal."

I asked him what he'd been eating, and he chuckled, "You know what hospital food is like, don't you?" I glanced at the uneaten lunch tray, wondering how sick he really was.

For the next few hours, we talked non-stop. We hadn't seen each other for a few years, so we had plenty of catching up to do. By evening, he was clearly getting tired, and I knew I would have to leave soon. It stilled seemed odd to me that Daddy was so alert and alive. "Aren't you hungry?" I asked him.

"You know what sounds good to me?" I couldn't imagine.

"I wish I had one of those pineapple pizzas." I shook my head in disbelief.

"I'll see if I can find one." I asked my stepmother

to come with me. We rushed out the door, hailed a cab and found a local pizza kitchen. Twenty minutes later, we were back, pizza in hand. I brought him his favorite kind of bottled ice tea, too, and hoped the combination wouldn't be too deadly.

My father had always been a heavy eater, so the sight of him pigging out on pizza wasn't all that shocking to me. But my stepmother could hardly believe her eyes. And when the doctor arrived, he stared at the old man as if he were seeing a mirage.

I left him two hours later, wondering how violently ill he was going to be. He called me the next day. "I'm going home," he told me. "They want my bed for some sick old man."

Daddy was at home for another six months until the cancer caught up with him again. He died peacefully in his sleep, and I had no chance to get back up to see him before his death. But my last memories of him will last as long as I do. I can still see the grin on his face when I walked into the room and the light in his eyes when the pineapple pizza and ice tea appeared on his bedside table.

J. M.,
Cedarhurst, NY

$\mathcal{L}$osing your mom is a gigan-
tic tragedy when you're little. I was just starting junior high when my mother died of cancer, so my emotions were already intense and unpredictable. We went through the surgeries and chemotherapy treatments on a day to day basis, but I was so upset that my grades dropped and I kind of turned into a loner. I even experimented with drugs and alcohol. Most of all, I just didn't care if I lived or died. I think I would have become suicidal if it hadn't been for my dad.

Once Mom was gone, he did everything in his power to help me get back on track. My brothers were already gone away to college, so Dad just focused on me and my needs. He was incredible. He talked to me constantly. He made me breakfast everyday. He took me out to eat at nice restaurants. He planned weekend trips and activities so I always had some time to look forward to. He bought me surprises and came to all my school activities, even if it meant he had to miss meetings at work or rearrange his schedule. Before long, my outlook started to improve, and by the time I started high school, I was enjoying life again.

Then the worst happened. Dad got sick, too.

By the middle of my junior year in high school, we pretty well knew that he wasn't going to make it. I was always emotionally bonded with my dad, and even more so since Mom's death. And now I would be all alone

Dad was a man of strong faith, and he made me promise him that I would trust God and let him be my father once he was gone. Although I couldn't understand God's will in allowing both my parents to die, I knew that I needed God to help me. And he has.

Dad won't be there to walk me down the aisle when I get married like I always dreamed he would. But in some way I really don't understand, I feel his presence every day, and his memory lives on in my heart and soul. The love my Dad showed me when I needed it most saved my life, and it changed me forever. I'll always love him.

J. F.,
Oxford, MS

$\mathcal{T}$rying to talk to my mother was never easy. And when the subject of my father was raised, well, you could just forget trying to find anything out at all.

All my life I wanted to know him. He was an obsession to me, a fantasy. When my mother yelled at me or hit me, I went to my room and dreamed about a time when I would meet my father and he would be kind to me. When she left me alone at night, I called information in every city I could think of, hoping to track him down. I didn't know much, but I knew his name and I knew he'd wanted to take me away from her when I was two years old. That's just about all I needed to hear. I was pretty sure Mom didn't love me. Maybe he did.

When I was fourteen, I started hanging around

with some pretty wild kids. I never really got into drugs the way they did, and I could see that some of their decisions were pretty stupid. But one thing I learned from them was how to survive on the street. By the time I was sixteen, I was pretty sure I knew what I was doing, and I decided to run away from home and find my dad.

By then, I'd heard from my Grandma that he was in Seattle. I'd saved up some money, and I took a bus from Northern California to Portland. I hitched the rest of the way. Looking back, I can see that I was pretty lucky. The people who gave me rides were nice, and nobody tried to take advantage of me.

Once I got to Seattle, I went to a pay phone and called the number I had. A man answered. I told him who I was, and he sounded pretty choked up. He said he'd be there to pick me up within a half-hour. I was really nervous by then. I knew I looked terrible, and I wondered if he'd take one look at me and send me back to Mom.

He didn't.

Instead, he cried when he saw me. He'd brought his wife with him, and she cried too. She told me they'd been praying for me for years, and that this was, for them, an answered prayer. That night they made me call Mom and tell her I was alright. Then they told me I could stay if I wanted to.

That was the beginning of the best two years of my life. I changed so much once I went to live with Dad that I wouldn't have recognized myself. He and my step-mom were strong Christians. They went to church and they firmly believed that God had done a miracle by bringing me to them. That made me feel more loved than I'd ever felt before—not only by them but also by God.

Dad died two years later. I guess he'd had heart trouble for a long time. But by then, I was ready to go on to college and make a life of my own. I've been able to build a better relationship with Mom since then too, although I don't think she'll ever forgive me for wanting to live with Dad and his wife. Most of all, I'm just thankful. I think I knew all along that Dad would love me and welcome me if I could just find him. Maybe that's why I couldn't let go of my dream.

M. R.,
Renton, WA

*I*t could be said that my father fought and lost a battle with a debilitating disease. He is no longer living, but he left behind a wealth of memories. The things I remember are visions of a man who loved me as long as he lived . . .

I see him striding through the cornfield, hands in his pockets, inspecting his crops.

I see him strolling along the city sidewalk, smiling at everyone he passed.

I see him proudly displaying a prize deer he shot on his annual hunting trip, his tiny daughter nestled at his side.

I see him pointing out the dew to me as it glistened on the morning grass.

I see him gently shushing me, so I wouldn't miss the bird's song.

I see him talking to me long into the night, our conversations stretching into the wee hours of the morning, constructing a sound foundation of knowledge and wisdom.

I see him chasing me though a clover field on a sunny summer day.

I see him patiently explaining something to me, his laughter ringing through the air.

I see him fighting for his life in the hospital, never complaining, and never giving up.

And now that the battle is over, he lives on in my heart and mind and in my memories.

S. K.,
Elgin, IL

Part 7

. . . Like the wind, the years go by.

Precious butterfly, spread your wings and fly.

❧

Allowing our little girls to test their wings and leave
the nest is one of the hardest things dads ever have to
do. We've been so committed to protecting, nurturing,
guiding, and teaching our daughters that our relation–
ship with them seems to be coming to an end when it's
finally time for them to go. How can we release them
to experience hurts, failures, and disappointments?
How can we entrust them to the very world we've
sheltered them from for a couple of decades? We get all
torn up at the prospect, and our only recourse is to

give them up to God, and believe that He will continue to father them, even when we can't be there to help Him out.

*W*hen I learned that Clare was getting married, I was genuinely happy for her. She had met a good-looking, successful young man, and it looked to me as if they really cared about each other. I'd been her stepfather since she was five years old, and assumed that she would want me to walk her down the aisle. Nothing could have made me happier than that—she was my pride and joy.

Clare's father had rarely visited her, almost never called her, and hadn't paid more than $100 child support in fifteen years. He was a nice enough guy, but his immaturity and lack of responsibility had always offended me. Here was this beautiful, intelligent young daughter of his, and as far as I could see, he didn't want to give her the time of day.

I'd noticed that, as she got older, Clare had tried

to find common ground with her father. I knew she loved me and would always appreciate the care I'd given her and the love I felt for her. But something inside her longed to be loved and accepted by her "real" dad. Part of me understood. Another part of me was hurt.

So you can imagine how I felt when she told me that she wanted "him" to walk down the aisle with her and me. One of us would be on one side, one on the other. I recoiled from the idea. I was hurt and offended. What right did he have to share that special day with her? I had seen her through thick and thin. I had advised her about her boyfriend, now her fiancé. And, if that weren't enough, I was paying for the wedding!

I bristled as we talked. First I objected. Then I got quiet, and bit my tongue. Finally, she took my hand and said, "You're my Daddy. That's who you are and that's who you always will be. But this man has a little place in my life too, and I don't want to hurt him. He's a damaged, selfish person. But he's still my flesh and blood, and since he's alive and in touch with me, I want him to have a part in my wedding. Do you understand?"

"Not exactly. But I won't make any trouble for you. You know that . . ."

"That's not the point, Daddy. This is an act of kindness toward a lonely, lost man. Can't you see that?"

"It's humiliating to me," I said.

"Why? Because you taught me to be kind, and now I'm being kind? Because you taught me to forgive, and now I'm forgiving? Why are you humiliated? If it weren't for all the things you've taught me, I wouldn't be able to do it."

Of course she'd won. And just before the wedding, an interesting thing happened. Her birth father called me aside, and he thanked me for everything I'd done for her. His eyes were actually teary, and he said, "You did what I should have done, and I thank

you. You've been a great dad to her. I owe you one—
a big one."

That helped a lot. But at the reception, when it
was time for the father–daughter dance, Clare took my
arm. She looked more beautiful than she knew. And
without a look at anyone else, without even a glance at
"him," she danced the whole dance with me. The song
we danced to was "Butterfly Kisses."

I glanced at her mother, and she was crying. As
a matter of fact, so was I.

J. G.,
Jefferson City, MS

*M*y daughter and I used to share a fairly typical father–daughter relationship. I teased her, criticized her boyfriends and yelled at her when she was learning how to drive. The rest of her upbringing I left to her mother, who knew a lot more about the ways of women than I did.

When my daughter was a senior in high school, however, her mother was killed by a drunk driver. And from that day forward, things were very different for both of us. At first, we hung on to each other for comfort. We cried together at the hospital, we cried at the funeral, and sometimes we cried just sitting at home.

As we tried to get used to my wife's loss, my daughter began to confide in me the things she used to tell her mother. At first I felt completely inadequate—I thought I had to have an answer for everything. But I soon learned that she just needed to talk to me, and to know I cared. So I started listening more and making less suggestions. And she seemed fine with that.

I think the one thing I helped her see was that every problem we face isn't necessarily as huge as we may think at first. Sometimes we make problems bigger than they really are, and we suffer unnecessarily. Other times our problems really are big. And that's when we need to help carry each other's burdens. The biggest burden either of us has ever faced has been learning to live without her mother. We would have never made it without each other.

Last year my daughter graduated from college, and she's about to begin law school. I'm so proud of her. She's had to overcome a lot, and she's done it so well. She's become mature and trustworthy. I realized the other day that I couldn't wait to get home to talk over a work situation with her. I've learned to value her opinion, just as she's come to appreciate mine.

After all we've been through, my daughter has become one of my confidants, just as I've become one of hers.

R. F.,
Lubbock, TX

*M*y daughter Vicky was twelve years old when she phoned me. I still find it hard to believe that she found the courage to get my number and make the call. For me, it was a miracle.

Vicky's mother and I divorced when she was just a baby. There were so many fights—so much screaming, so many ugly words. I tried to take Vicky with me, but her mother became violent and threatened to hurt her. So I left. I was only eighteen at the time and didn't really know what to do except get away and hope that Vicky would be all right. I guess I thought that if I weren't there, the trouble would stop.

Well, it didn't.

Vicky was verbally and physically abused by her mother all her life. And when she called me, my heart nearly broke. I had never remarried and was living alone. I called my mom and dad and asked if they agreed that I should go get her. They agreed. So the three of us went to my ex-wife's house and picked Vicky up. She was bruised and had welts on her back. She was terrified of what might happen, but we had already worked things out with the authorities by the time we got there.

Vicky came to live with me, and at first we were like two strangers, even though she was my daughter. But we got to know each other a little better every day, and I could see her beginning to relax as the weeks passed. She went to my parents' house after school, and I picked her up after I finished my teaching job at the local high school.

It wasn't long before we were really enjoying each other's company. I guess I'd been lonelier than I'd realized, and she was so happy just to be with some-one who cared about her and didn't fly off the handle.

She told me one day that her mother had said a lot

of bad things about me—I wasn't really surprised—and that she was surprised at how nice I was and how different I was from what she had expected. She said, "I like it when you make me laugh—it helps me feel less stressed out." She hasn't said so, but I think kidding around and teasing her has eased her pain and helped her feel more positive.

There has always been laughter in our home ever since she came. We've learned a lot about dealing with the past. It hasn't always been easy—my ex-wife tried to take Vicky away from me more than once. But Vicky has now reached fourteen. In our state that means that she can choose where she will live. And she wants to live with me. My parents helped me find a counselor she could talk to about her experiences with her mother, and it has helped her a lot just to put into words some of the feelings she's faced.

Last Father's Day, she wrote me a note: "Dad, I want you to know that I not only love you, but I admire and respect you, too. You've taught me more than I could ever learn from books, and you've also helped me see how important education is. I've learned so much from you, and I have decided to become a teacher like you. Thanks for being there, and for being who you are. Love, Vicky."

W. G.,
Santa Barbara, CA

$\mathcal{T}$here are a lot of ways to say "I love you." My dad wasn't one to put his feelings into words, but in so many other ways, he has let me know that he loves me. One of the ways that means the most to me is that he has always given me a chance to try anything I wanted to try. After teaching me the how-tos, he would also give me warnings about what not to try to do myself.

For example, when I got my driver's license, my dad taught me how to change all four tires and taught me which fluids I needed to check and fill, if necessary. Once he was satisfied that I knew how to manage on my own, he handed me the car keys, and opened the car door for me. "Now you can take care of yourself."

Impatient to be on my way, I thanked him, rolled up the window and started to back out of the driveway.

Dad tapped on the window. I stopped. "I wasn't fin-ished," he explained.

"If you ever do break down along the road, DO NOT EVER get out of the car. Lock the doors. If somebody stops to help you, roll the window down one inch and give them one of these."

Dad handed me what look like a matchbook. But instead of being full of matches, it had sheets of paper inside, and every little sheet was printed with his name, his work phone number and our home phone number.

"Just tell them to call me," he said. "And I'll be there right away."

K. C.,

Elizabethtown, KY

The stereotypical "dad" you hear about is a guy who is always at work, always playing golf, always busy, and never around for his kids. My dad was never like that. He was with me as much as possible, and he seemed to love every minute of it. He taught me to ride a bike, provided a shoulder to cry on, and bolstered my confidence before my first date. He always explained things to me, and he took a lot of time to communicate, which is something some fathers apparently never learn to do.

Still, one of the great lessons of my life came from watching him, not from listening to him. I learned the most about my dad's character when he lost his job. He had worked at the same company for twenty-five years, as long as I could remember, when downsizing cost him his position. Terrible as the blow was to his self-confidence, he never missed a beat. Every morning afterwards he got up, put on a coat and tie, and headed out to look for work.

He went to headhunter agencies. He answered classified ads. He called on his friends. For several weeks, he came up with nothing. He was clearly disappointed, but he didn't complain, and he didn't blame anybody. He just kept looking.

When he finally found a new job, it didn't pay as much as his old one. So he took a second job, and soon he was working fifteen-hour days. He also worked all weekend, so he never had a day off. For the first time in our lives, Dad wasn't around very much. We missed him terribly, but if he wasn't going to complain, neither were we.

After trying to keep up this pace for more than a year, my dad called us all into the dining room for a family meeting. He told us that he wanted to try to start his own business. He knew it would be challenging, but he thought he could make a go of it. He was afraid, but he had the courage to try. And when he succeeded, nobody was surprised.

As wonderful as my father has always been in so many loving and sensitive ways, his determination and tenacity are the things I admire most about him. He never told me not to give up, but by his example he showed me how to keep going. During a particularly difficult semester in college, I really toyed with the idea of quitting. But I didn't even mention it to Dad. It wasn't that he'd disapprove. It was just that he would never have quit himself, and I thought he deserved the same kind of effort from me.

K. E.,
Ashland, OR

*M*y dad and I didn't start out very well. I never saw him when I was a little kid, and I guess I resented that fact that his job came first. He was always too busy to be at my school events, my soccer games, my music recitals, or whatever else I did. He was a successful man, so we lived well, and maybe I didn't appreciate him enough for that. But I just wanted a dad who cared, and I felt like I didn't matter to him. I know now that my mom felt like she didn't matter to him either.

But then, when I was seventeen, we got a phone call from the East Coast (we live in California) that Dad was in the hospital. He'd had a major heart attack and would have to have bypass surgery. Mom went back to be with him and brought him back home after the operation. For a while, during his recuperation, I don't think Dad knew whether he would live or die. It was a turning point in our lives.

Dad had to take a lot of time off work, and he was always home. For the first time ever, we got to know each other. He actually got interested in what I did, what I thought, and who I am. And I guess the more he cared about me, the more I started to care about him. Dad went back to work after he was fully recovered, but he never was married to his job again. Maybe he had time to think about what really mattered, or maybe he just got to know us. I know he and Mom seemed like they really loved each other after that.

About three years later, I went through my own problems. I got married at eighteen, and in less than a year, I knew it wasn't going to work out at all. My husband was really mean to me, and after he hit me a couple of times, I asked my dad if I could come home. He showed up with a U-Haul truck a few hours later and helped me move back in.

Dad stood by me through that whole, awful

experience. He used to say, "Honey, someday you're going to have a new and better life with someone wonderful. You just wait."

He was right. I'm getting married this fall, and the man I'm marrying is really wonderful. Just like my Dad.

J. D.,
Vista, CA

*W*hen you think about it, parents have a pretty strange job. They are given their beautiful children to care for, teach, and love. And good parents do everything in their power to build a strong family so the kids can grow up in a healthy and happy environment. But the parents' real purpose is to prepare their children to leave that family, to strike out on their own, to be independent. And when that day finally comes, it feels like a tragedy, not a success story.

My wife struggled for six months with the imminent departure of our oldest daughter. At times I thought she was overreacting just a little. As Gayle visited campuses, researched universities, and filled out college applications, her mom expressed a sense of impending doom. "It almost feels like someone's dying," she tried to explain. "Our family will never be the same."

I patted her arm, smiled condescendingly, and thought to myself, "Women!"

Then came the day of Gayle's departure. We had shipped most of her stuff across the country by truck, and now she was waiting at the departure gate with her bags, just minutes away from boarding the plane. All at once I was overwhelmed by a huge tide of emotion. I looked at my daughter standing there, and she still seemed like a child to me. How could she go so far away from home? Who would take care of her? How could she be on her own, without us there to listen, to laugh, and to pray with her? How could she be leaving us? How could I let her go?

I was trying to give her some last minute advice when my throat choked up, and I couldn't say another word. I stifled it momentarily, but tears were soon pouring down my face. Before I could stop myself, I was holding her in my arms and sobbing. By now she was crying too.

Looking back, I think it was one of the hardest days of my life. My little girl was on her way to chase her own dreams and find her own life. We had been good parents. We had loved her, honored her, and protected her as best we could. And now she was gone. Just like that. Fortunately my wife was far more understanding than I had been. She was right all along. Our family would never be the same again.

D. S.,

Fort Worth, TX

Dad and I could always talk about things, and we even talked about the time when I would leave and strike out on my own. I was an independent girl, and Dad wasn't a possessive father, so we both understood that I would one day make a life of my own.

I dated a hometown boy on and off throughout college, and it always seemed as if we would get married and build a future together. But one weekend I got the news that he had met someone else, was madly in love with her, and didn't want to see me anymore. This was an enormous blow to me—somehow, without realizing it, I had included him in all my plans, all my dreams, and all my goals. I was more devastated than I could ever have imagined.

For several weeks, I fought depression, and although I wanted to talk things over with Dad, I just couldn't find the words. When Dad finally decided we needed to talk, his words came as quite a surprise. I had expected a pep talk—"You can do it—get out there and catch the world by the tail." But Dad wanted to say something else, something that, at the time, meant more to me than any cheerleading he might have done.

He sat down next to me, and he took my hand in his, "Honey, I don't expect to take care of you for the rest of my life. I don't think that's going to happen. But I just want you to know something—I will, if you need me to." As Dad's words sank into my heart, I realized that he had said exactly just the right words. I would never be "dependent" on him, and he knew it. But if I needed a place to live, a strong support, or a shoulder to cry on, he'd be there.

These days I'm a successful and financially secure woman. But underneath me, I always know there's a safety net, a pair of loving arms that will catch me if I fall. That was all I needed to know so I could dare to try my wings.

V. B.,
New Washington, IN

*M*y memories of Daddy are farm memories. The smell of wheat fields, of hickory smoke, of fresh-plowed earth will always make me think of him. Daddy was a fifth-generation farmer, and he had no boys to carry on his heritage. Since I was his oldest daughter, he tried to teach me everything he could about farming.

From my fifth birthday on, I rode the combine with him. I helped him out in the barn. I rode alongside him in the pick-up as he bounced along dirt roads to survey the progress of the crops. I knew that he dreamed of handing over the farm to me when I was grown, but deep in my heart, farming wasn't what I wanted to do.

Instead, I went away to college, got my degree, and struck out on my own. Dad was disappointed, and for a few years he didn't talk to me about much besides the weather and the relatives. Meanwhile, I built my own business from the ground up, and before long I was doing very well in both reputation and finance.

One morning, bright and early, my assistant informed me that my father was on the phone. I quickly realized that he'd never called me at work before, and my first thought was that something had happened to Mom. But, to my amazement, he had something else in mind. "I've got some financial decisions to make here," he explained. "You know more about this kind of thing than I do. How about coming by the house tonight and telling me what you think about these papers I'm supposed to sign?"

From that day on, Dad counted on me as his financial advisor. I think, in a way, it makes him feel as if I were part of the family business after all. And it makes me happy, after we've talked through all his concerns, to walk outside with him—through the wheat fields and over to the barn. I've got the best of both worlds.

M. P.,
Mayfield, KY

*M*y father was thrilled when I told him I was getting married. He even seemed excited about the wedding itself, and I wondered if he had even the slightest idea what he was getting into. My mother had died several years before, and I knew that without her very capable help, putting a wedding together wasn't going to be easy. Dad was more than willing to help, but he was a scientist— a chemist, to be exact—and I couldn't imagine him serving as a wedding coordinator. As it turned out, I couldn't have been more mistaken.

After Mom's death, her business had gone downhill, and we didn't have much money. I wanted to invite three hundred people to the wedding, and I told Dad that we'd just keep things simple and inexpensive—not to worry about the finances. I thought he understood, but the next thing I knew, he was on the phone to every person we knew, every church in the neighborhood, every musician we'd ever met. Dad was on a roll, and nothing could stop him.

Dad borrowed tables, and somebody loaned him white linen tablecloths and napkins. He bargained for flowers, and with the help of relatives, he decorated the church, our house, and all the tables. Dad recruited cooks and supervised the creation of a delicious menu. He located four "volunteers" from a local university to perform as a string quartet—they just happened to be symphony players. He interviewed distant cousins who were potential bakers and cake decorators. He took me china shopping, dress ordering, and honeymoon scheduling.

By the time he was finished, Dad was the executive producer of a candle-lit wedding ceremony in a flower-strewn church, a performance of world-class music, a festive, gourmet-quality reception luncheon, a perfectly timed limousine ride to the airport, and a fabulous honeymoon trip.

At the end of the day, as we kissed him goodbye, Dad turned to me with tears in his eyes. "I'm sorry, sweetheart," he said apologetically. "I just wish I could have afforded the kind of wedding you deserve."

J. H.,
Greensboro, NC

*W*hen I was a young man, I used to play the guitar and sing, and people were kind enough to tell me that I was rather good at it. I played at church functions, and occasionally for a wedding or family event. As a child, my little daughter always seemed proud of my amateur performances. I enjoyed watching her face light up when I appeared guitar in hand, in front of a group of people.

But as the years went by, life got busier and busier, and the old guitar collected a lot of dust. I rarely got it out and played it, and when I did, I was always surprised at how rusty my fingers were and how terrible my voice sounded to me. The less I played and sang, the more self-conscious I became.

My daughter grew up and got married, and now she has a son of her own. One night, when she and her